D1154652

The Wright's Chaste Wife.

Early English Text Society
Original Series, No. 12

The

𝔚right's ℭhaste 𝔚ife,

OR

"A Fable of a wryght that was maryde to a pore
wydows dowtre / the whiche wydow havyng
noo good to geve with her / gave as for
a precyous Johell to hym a Rose
garlond / the whyche sche affermyd
wold never fade while sche
kept truly her wedlok."

A Merry Tale, by Adam of Cobsam,

*From a MS. in the Library of the Archbishop of Canterbury,
at Lambeth, about 1462 A.D.*

COPIED AND EDITED BY

FREDERICK J. FURNIVALL.

GREENWOOD PRESS, PUBLISHERS
NEW YORK

Originally published in 1865 and 1886
by Oxford Universities Press

First Greenwood Reprinting 1969

SBN 8371-1776-3

PREFACE.

Good wine needs no bush, and this tale needs no Preface.
I shall not tell the story of it—let readers go to the verse
itself for that; nor shall I repeat to those who begin it the
exhortation of the englisher of *Sir Generides,*

> "for goddes sake, or ye hens wende,
> Here this tale unto the ende."—(ll. 3769-70.)

If any one having taken it up is absurd enough to lay it
down without finishing it, let him lose the fun, and let all
true men pity him. Though the state of morals disclosed by
the story is not altogether satisfactory, yet it is a decided
improvement on that existing in Roberd of Brunne's time in
1303, for he had to complain of the lords of his day:

> Also do þese lordynges,
> þe[y] trespas moche yn twey þynges;
> þey rauys a mayden aȝens here wyl,
> And mennys wyuys þey lede awey þertyl.
> A grete vylanye þarte he dous
> Ȝyf he make therof hys rouse [boste]:
> þe dede ys confusyun,
> And more ys þe dyffamacyun.

The volume containing the poem was shown to me by Mr
Stubbs, the Librarian at Lambeth, in order that I might see
the version of Sir Gyngelayne, son of Sir Gawain, which Mr
Morris is some day, I trust, to edit for the Society in one of
his Gawain volumes.[1] Finding the present poem also on the
paper leaves, I copied it out the same afternoon, and here it
is for a half-hour's amusement to any reader who chooses to
take it up.

The handwriting of the MS. must be of a date soon after
1460, and this agrees well with the allusion to Edward the
Fourth's accession, and the triumph of the White Rose o'er the
Red alluded to in the last lines of the poem.   The Garlond,

> It was made . . .
> Of flourys most of honoure,
> Of roses whyte þat wyłł nott fade,
> Whych floure ałł ynglond doth glade. . .
> Vn-to the whych floure I-wys
> The loue of God and of the comonys
> Subdued bene of ryght.

For, that the Commons of England were glad of their
Yorkist king, and loved Duke Richard's son, let Holinshed's
record prove.   He testifies :

"Wherevpon it was againe demanded of the commons, if they
would admit and take the said erle as their prince and souereigne
lord; which all with one voice cried: Yea, yea. . .

"Out of the ded stocke sprang a branch more mightie than the
stem; this Edward the Fourth, a prince so highlie fauoured of the
peple, for his great liberalitie, clemencie, vpright dealing, and courage,
that aboue all other, he with them stood in grace alone: by reason
whereof, men of all ages and degrees to him dailie repaired, some
offering themselues and their men to ioepard their liues with him,
and other plentiouslie gaue monie to support his charges, and to
mainteine his right."

---

[1] The since printing of the Romance in the Percy Folio MS. Ballads and
Romances, (*Lybius Disconius*, ii. 404,) will probably render this unnecessary.
(1869.)

Would that we knew as much of Adam of Cobsam as of our White-Rose king. He must have been one of the Chaucer breed,[1] but more than this poem tells of him I cannot learn.

3, *St George's Square, N.W.*,
    23 *November*, 1865.

P.S.—There are other Poems about Edward IV. in the volume, which will be printed separately.[2] One on Women is given at the end of the present text.

PP.S. 1869.—Mr C. H. Pearson, the historian of the Early and Middle Ages of England, has supplied me with the immediate original of this story. He says:

"The Wright's Chaste Wife is a reproduction of one of the *Gesta Romanorum*, cap. 69, de Castitate, ed. Keller. The Latin story begins 'Gallus regnavit prudens valde.' The Carpenter gets a shirt with his wife, which is never to want washing unless one of them is unfaithful. The lovers are three Knights (*milites*), and they are merely kept on bread and water, not made to work; nor is any wife introduced to see her lord's discomfiture. The English version, therefore, is much quainter and fuller of incident than its original. But the 'morality' of the Latin story is rich beyond description. 'The wife is holy Mother Church,' 'the Carpenter is the good Christian,' 'the shirt is our Faith, because, as the apostle says, it is impossible to please God without faith.' The Wright's work typifies 'the building up the pure heart by the works of mercy.' The three Knights are 'the pride of life, the lust of the eyes, and the lust of the flesh.' 'These you must shut up in the chamber of penance till you get an eternal reward from the eternal King.' 'Let us therefore pray God,' &c."

With the Wright's Chaste Wife may also be compared the stories mentioned in the Notes, p. 20, and the Ballad "The Fryer well fitted; or

---

[1] Chaucer brings off his Carpenter, though, triumphant, and not with the swived wife and broken arm that he gives his befooled Oxford craftsman in *The Milleres Tale*. (1869.)

[2] In *Political, Religious, and Love Poems*, E. E. Text Soc., 1867.

> A Pretty jest that once befel,
> How a maid put a Fryer to cool in the well"

printed "in the Bagford Collection; in the Roxburghe (ii. 172); the Pepys (iii. 145); the Douce (p. 85); and in *Wit and Mirth, an Antidote to Melancholy*, 8vo. 1682; also, in an altered form, in Pills to purge Melancholy, 1707, i. 340; or 1719, iii. 325"; and the tune of which, with an abstract of the story, is given in Chappell's *Popular Music*, i. 273-5. The Friar makes love to the Maid; she refuses him for fear of hell-fire.

> Tush, quoth the Friar, thou needst not doubt;
> If thou wert in Hell, I could sing thee out.

So she consents if he'll bring her an angel of money. He goes home to fetch it, and she covers the well over with a cloth. When he comes back, and has given her the money, she pretends that her father is coming, tells the Friar to run behind the cloth, and down he flops into the well. She won't help him at first, because if he could sing her out of hell, he can clearly sing himself out of the well; but at last she does help him out, keeps his money because he's dirtied the water, and sends him home dripping along the street like a new-washed sheep.

THE WRIGHT'S CHASTE WIFE.

[*MS. Lambeth* 306, *leaves* 178-187.]

Aꝇmyghty god, maker of all*e*,
Saue you my sou*e*reyns in towre & hall*e*, My sovereigns,
3 And send yoū good grace !
If ye wyꝇ a stounde blynne,
Of a story I wyꝇ begynne, I will tell you a
6 And telle you ·aꝇ the cas, tale
Meny farleyes þat I haue herd*e*,
Ye would haue wondyr how yt ferde ;
9 Lystyn, and ye schaꝇ here ;
Of a wryght I wyꝇ you telle, of a wright
That some tyme in thys land gan dwelle, of this land,
12 And lyued by hys myster.
Whether that he were yn or owte, who, at work, was
Of erthely man hadde he no dowte, afraid of no
  earthly man.
15 To werke hows, harowe, nor plowgh,
Or other werkes, what so they were,
Thous wrought he hem farre and nere,
18 And dyd tham wele I-nough.
Thys wryght would wedde no wyfe, At first he would
Butt yn yougeth to lede hys lyfe wed no wife,
21 In myrthe and oþer melody ; [leaf 178, back]
Ou*er* aꝇ where he gan wende, for wherever he
Aꝇ they seyd " welcome, frende, went he was
  welcome ;
24 Sytt downe, and do gla[d]ly."

but at last he
wished

Tyll on a tyme he was wyllyng,

As tyme comyth of alle thyng,

27 (So seyth the profesye,)

to have a spouse
to look after his
goods.

A wyfe for to wedde & haue

That myght hys goodes kepe and saue,

30   And for to leue all foly.

A widow near had
a fair daughter

Ther dwellyd a wydowe in þat contre

That hadde a doughter feyre & fre ;

33   Of her, word sprang wyde,

true and
meek.

For sche was bothe stabyll & trewe,

Meke of maners, and feyr' of hewe ;

36   So seyd men in that tyde.

The wryght seyde, " so god me saue,

Her the wright
would like to lie
by him,

Such a wyfe would I haue

39   To lye nyghtly by my syde."

He þought to speke wyth þat may,

and therefore
went to her
mother

And rose erly on a daye

42   And þyder gan he to ryde.

The wryght was welcome to þe wyfe,

And her saluyd all so blyve,

45   And so he dyd her doughter fre :

and proposed for
the maiden.

For the erand that he for cam

Tho he spake, þat good yeman) ;

48   Than to hym seyd sche :

The mother says
she can only
give him as a
portion

The wydowe seyd, " by heuen kyng,

I may geue wyth her no þing,

51   (And þat forthynketh me ;)

a garland

Saue a garlond I wyll the geue,

Ye schall neuer see, whyle ye lyve,

54   None such in thys contre :

of roses

Haue here thys garlond of roses ryche,

In all thys lond ys none yt lyche,

that will keep its
colour
[leaf 179]

57   For ytt wyll euer be newe,

Wete þou wele withowtyn fable,

while his wife is
true,

All the whyle thy wyfe ys stable

60   The chaplett wolle hold hewe ;

And yf thy wyfe vse putry,

Or tolle eny man to lye her by,

63   Than wolle yt change hewe,

And by the garlond þou may see,

Fekyłł or fals yf þat sche be,

66   Or ellys yf sche be trewe."

Of thys chaplett hym was fułł fayne,

And of hys wyfe, was nott to layne ;

69   He weddyd her fułł sone,

And ladde her home wyth solempnite,

And hyld her brydałł dayes thre.

72   Whan they home come,

Thys wryght in hys hart cast,

If that he walkyd est or west

75   As he was wonte to done,

"My wyfe þat ys so bryght of ble,

Men wolle desyre her' fro me,

78   And þat hastly and sone ;"

Butt sone he hym byþought

That a chambyr schuld be wrought

81   Bothe of lyme and stone,

Wyth wallys strong as eny stele,

And dorres sotylly made and wele,

84   He owte framyd yt sone ;

The chambyr he lett make fast,

Wyth plaster of parys þat wyłł last,

87   Such ous know I neuer none ;

Ther ys [ne] kyng ne emperoure,

And he were lockyn in þat towre,

90   That cowde gete owte of þat wonne.

Nowe hath he done as he þought,

And in the myddes of the flore wrought

93   A wondyr strange gyle,

A trapdoure rounde abowte

That no man myght come yn nor owte ;

96   It was made wyth a wyle,

but change when
she is faithless.

The wright is
delighted with his
garland and wife,

marries her
and takes her
home ;

and then begins
to think that
when he is out at
work

men will try to
corrupt his wife.

So he plans a
crafty room and
tower,

and builds it soon
with plaster of
Paris,

which no one
could ever get out
of if he once got
into it,

for there was a
trapdoor in the
middle,

[leaf 179, back]

and if any one
only touched it,
down he'd go into
a pit.

That who-so touchyd yt eny thyng,

In to þe pytt he schuld flyng

99   Wythyn a lytyll whyle.

This was to stop
any tricks with
his wife.

For hys wyfe he made that place,

That no man schuld beseke her of grace,

102   Nor her to begyle.

Just then the
town Lord

By þat tyme þe lord of the towne

Hadde ordeynyd tymbyr redy bowne,

105   An halle to make of tre.

sends for him to
build a Hall,

After the wryght the lord lett sende,

For þat he schuld wyth hym lende

(a job for two or
three months,)

108   Monythys two or thre.

The lord seyd, " woult þou haue þi wyfe?

and offers to
fetch his wife too.

I wyll send after her blyve

111   That sche may com to the."

The wryght hys garlond hadde take wyth hym,

That was bryght and no þing dymme,

114   Yt wes feyre on to see.

He sees the
wright's garland,
and asks what it
means.

The lord axyd hym as he satt,

" Felowe, where hadyst þou þis hatte

117   That ys so feyre and newe ? "

The wryght answerd all so blyue,

" Sir, it will

And seyd, " syr, I hadde yt wyth my wyfe,

120   And þat dare me neuer' rewe ;

tell me whether
my wife is false
or true;

Syr, by my garlond I may see

Fekyll or fals yf þat sche be,

[¹ MS. of]

123   Or¹ yf þat sche be trewe ;

and will change
its colour if she
go wrong."

And yf my wyfe loue a paramoure,

Than wyll my garlond vade coloure,

126   And change wyll yt the hewe."

The lord þought " by godys myght,

" I'll try that,"
thinks the Lord,

That wyll I wete thys same nyght

129   Whether thys tale be trewe."

and goes to the
wright's wife.

To the wryghtys howse anon he went,

He fonde the wyfe ther-in presente

132 That was so bryght and schene;   [leaf 180]
   Sone he hayled her trewly,
   And so dyd sche the lord curtesly :
135 Sche seyd, " welcome ye be ; "
   Thus seyd the wyfe of the hows,
   " Syr, howe faryth my swete spouse She asks after her husband,
138 That hewyth vppon your' tre ? "
   " Sertes, dame," he seyd, " wele, but the Lord
   And I am come, so haue I hele,
141 To wete the wylle of the ;
   My loue ys so vppon the cast declares his own love for her,
   That me thynketh my hert wolle brest,
144 It wolle none otherwyse be ;
   Good dame, graunt me thy grace and prays her to grant him his will.
   To pley with the in some preuy place
147 For gold and eke for fee."
   " Good syr, lett be youre fare, She entreats him to let that be,
   And of such wordes speke no mare
150 For hys loue þat dyed on tre ;
   Hadde we onys begonne þat gle,
   My husbond by his garlond myght see ;
153 For sorowe he would wexe woode."
   " Certes, dame," he seyd, " naye ; but he presses her,
   Loue me, I pray you, in þat ye maye :
156 For godys loue change thy mode,
   Forty marke schall be youre mede and offers her 40 marks.
   Of syluer and of gold[e] rede,
159 And that schall do the good."
   " Syr, that deede schall be done ; On this she consents if he'll put down the money.
   Take me that mony here anone."
162 " I swere by the holy rode
   I thought when I cam hydder'
   For to bryng[1] yt all to-gydder', [¹ or hyng. ? MS.]
165 As I mott broke my heele."
   Ther sche toke xl marke The 40 marks she takes,
   Of syluer and gold styff and sterke :

168 Sche toke yt feyre and welle ;

Sche seyd, " in to the chambyr wyll we,

Ther no man schall vs see ;

171 No lenger wyll we spare."

Vp the steyer they gan¹ hye :

The stepes were made so queyntly

174 That farther myght he nott fare.

The lord stumbyllyd as he went in hast,

He fell doune in to þat chaste

177 Forty fote and somedele more.

The lord began to crye ;

The wyfe seyd to hym in hye,

180 " Syr, what do ye there ? "

" Dame, I can nott seye howe

That I am come hydder nowe

183 To thys hows þat ys so newe ;

I am so depe in thys sure flore

That I ne can come owte att no dore ;

186 Good dame, on me þou rewe ! "

" Nay," sche seyd, " so mut y the,

Tyll myne husbond come and se,

189 I schrewe hym þat yt þought."

The lord arose and lokyd abowte

If he myght eny where gete owte,

192 Butt yt holpe hym ryght noght,

The wallys were so thycke wythyn,

That he no where myght owte wynne

195 But helpe to hym were brought ;

And euer the lord made euyll chere,

And seyd, " dame, þou schalt by thys dere."

198 Sche seyd that sche ne rought ;

Sche seyd " I recke nere

Whyle I am here and þou art there,

201 I schrewe herre þat þe doth drede."

The lord was sone owte of her þought,

The wyfe went in to her lofte,

¹ MS. gar

204   Sche satte and dyd her dede.

Than yt feſſ on þat oþer daye,

Of mete and drynke he gan her pray,

Next day the Lord begs for food.

207   There of he hadde gret nede.

He seyd, "dame, for seynt charyte,

Wyth some mete þou comfort me."

[leaf 181]

210   Sche seyd, "nay, so god me spede,

For I swere by swete seynt Iohne,

Mete ne drynke ne getyst þou none

" You'll get none from me

213   Butt þou wylt swete or swynke ;

For I haue both hempe and lyne,

And a betyngstocke fuſſ fyne,

unless you sweat for it," says she; "spin me some flax."

216   And a swyngyſſ good and grete ;

If þou wylt worke, tell me sone."

"Dame, bryng yt forthe, yt schaſſ be done,

He says he will :

219   Fuſſ gladly would I ete."

Sche toke the stocke in her honde,

And in to the pytt sche yt sclang

she throws him the tools,

222   Wyth a grete hete :

Sche brought the.lyne and hempe on her backe,

"Syr lord," sche seyd, "haue þou þat,

the flax and hemp, and says, " Work away."

225   And lerne for to swete."

Ther sche toke hym a bonde

For to occupy hys honde,

228   And bade hym fast on to bete.

He leyd yt downe on the[1] stone,

And leyd on strockes weſſ good wone,

[¹ ? MS. this.]   *He does, lays on well,*

231   And sparyd nott on to leyne.

Whan þat he hadde wrought a thraue,

Mete and drynke he gan to craue,

and then asks for his food,

234   And would haue hadde yt fayne ;

"That I hadde somewhat for to ete

Now after my gret swete ;

237   Me thynketh yt were rygſt,

For I haue labouryd nyght and daye

The for to plese, dame, I saye,

for he's toiled night and day.

240   And therto putt my myght."

The wife

The wyfe seyd " so mutt I haue hele,
And yf þi worke be wrought wele

243   Thou schalt haue to dyne."

gives him
meat and drink
[leaf 181, back]
and more flax,

Mete and drynke sche hym bare,
Wyth a thrafe of flex mare

246   Of full long boundyn lyne.

So feyre the wyfe the lord gan praye
That he schuld be werkyng aye,

and keeps him up
to his work.

249   And nought þat he schuld blynne ;

The lord was fayne to werke tho,
Butt hys men knewe nott of hys woo

252   Nor of þer lordes pyne.

The Steward asks
the wright after
his Lord,

The stuard to þe wryght gan saye,
" Sawe þou owte of my lord to-daye,

255   Whether that he ys wende ? "

The wryght answerde and seyd "naye ;
I sawe hym nott syth yesterdaye ;

258   I trowe þat he be schent."

then notices the
garland,

The stuard stode þe wryght by,
And of hys garlond hadde ferly

261   What þat yt be-mente.

and asks who
gave it him.

The stuard seyd, " so god me saue,
Of thy garlond wondyr I haue,

264   And who yt hath the sent."

"Sir, it will tell
me whether my
wife goes bad."

" Syr," he seyd, " be the same hatte
I can knowe yf my wyfe be badde

267   To me by eny other man) ;

If my floures ouþer fade or falle,
Then doth my wyfe me wrong wyth-alle,

270   As many a woman can)."

"I'll prove that
this very night,"
says the steward,

The stuard þought " by godes myght,
That schall I preue thys same nyght

273   Whether þou blys or banne,"

gets plenty of
money, and
goes off

And in to hys chambyr he gan gone,
And toke tresure full good wone,

276　　And forth he spedde hem than.

Butt he ne stynt att no stone

Tylł he vn-to þe wryghtes hows come

279　　That ylke same nyght.

He mett the wyfe amydde the gate,

Abowte þe necke he gan her take,

282　　And seyd " my dere wyght,

Ałł the good þat ys myne

I wyłł the geue to be thyne

285　　To lye by the ałł nyght."

Sche seyd, " syr, lett be thy fare,

My husbond wolle wete wyth-owtyn māre

288　　And I hym dyd that vnryght ;

I would nott he myght yt wete

For ałł the good that I myght gete,

291　　So Ihesus¹ mutt me spede

For, and eny man lay me by,

My husbond would yt wete truly,

294　　It ys wythowtyn eny drede."

The stuard seyd " for hym þat ys wrought,

There-of, dame, drede the noght

297　　Wyth me to do that dede ;

Haue here of me xx marke

Of gold and syluer styf and starke,

300　　Thys tresoure schałł be thy mede."

" Syr, and I graunt þat to yoū,

Lett no man wete butt we two nowe."

303　　He seyd, " nay, wythowtyn drede."

The stuard þought, ' sykerly

Women beth both queynte & slye.'

306　　The mony he gan her bede ;

He þought wele to haue be spedde,

And of his erand he was onredde

309　　Or he were fro hem I-gone.

Vp the sterys sche hym leyde

¹ MS. Ihc

2

to the wright's house,

takes her round the neck, and offers her all

[leaf 182]

he has, to lie by her that night.

She refuses,

as her husband would be sure to know of it.

The steward urges her again,

and offers her 20 marks.

She says, "Then don't tell any one,"

takes his money,

sends him up the quaint stairs,

Tyll he saw the wryghtes bedde :

312   Of tresoure þought he none ;

and lets him
tumble through
the trapdoor.

He went and stumblyd att a stone ;

In to þe seller' he fylle sone,

315   Downe to the bare flore.

The lord seyd " what deuyll art þoū ?

" What the devil
are you ? " says
the Lord.

And þou hadest falle on me nowe,

318   Thowe hadest hurt me full sore."

[leaf 182, back]

The stuard stert and staryd abowte

The steward finds
he can't get out ;

If he myght ower gete owte

321   Att hole lesse or mare.

The lord seyd, " welcome, and sytt be tyme,

For þou schalt helpe to dyght thys lyne

324   For all thy fers[e] fare."

The stuard lokyd on the knyght,

and wonders why
his Lord is there.

He seyd, " syr, for godes myght,

327   My lord, what do you here ? "

He seyd " felowe, wyth-owtyn oth,

" We both came
on one errand,
man."

For o erand we come bothe,

330   The sothe wolle I nott lete."

Tho cam the wyfe them vn-to,

The wife asks
what they're
doing ;

And seyd, " syres, what do you to,

333   Wyll ye nott lerne to swete ? "

Than seyd þe lord her vn-to,

the Lord says,

'Dame, your' lyne ys I-doo,

" Your flax is
done, and I want
my dinner."

336   Nowe would I fayne ete :

And I haue made yt all I-lyke,

Full clere, and no þing thycke,

339   Me thynketh yt gret payne."

The stuard seyd " wyth-owtyn dowte,

The steward says
if he ever gets out
he'll crack
her skull.

And euer I may wynne owte,

342   I wyll breke her brayne."

" Felowe, lett be, and sey nott so,

But the wife
chaffs him,

For þou schalt worke or euer þou goo,

says he'll soon be
glad to eat
his words,

345   Thy wordes þou torne agayne,

Fayne þou schalt be so to doo,

And thy good wylle put þerto ;

348 As a man buxome and bayne

Thowe schalt rubbe, rele, and spynne, *and unless he*

And þou wolt eny mete wynne, *rubs and reels,*

  he'll get no meat.

351 That I geue to god a gyfte."

The stuard seyd, "then haue I wondyr ; *" I'll die for*

Rather would I dy for hungyr *hunger first,*

  unhouseled,"

354 Wyth-owte hosyłł or shryfte." *answers he.*

The lord seyd, "so haue I hele,

Thowe wylt worke, yf þou hungyr welle, [leaf 183]

357 What worke þat the be brought."

The lord satt and dyd hys werke, *The Lord*

The stuard drewe in to the derke, *works away,*

360 Gret sorowe was in hys þought.

The lord seyd, " dame, here ys youre lyne,

Haue yt in godes blessyng and myne,

363 I hold yt welle I-wrought."

Mete and drynke sche gaue hym yn), *and gets his*

" The stuard," sche seyd, " wolle he nott spynne, *food and drink.*

366 Wyłł he do ryght noght ?"

The lord seyd, " by swete sen Ione,

Of thys mete schałł he haue none *None of it will he*

369 That ye haue me hydder brought." *give to the*

  steward,

The lord ete and dranke fast, *but eats it all up,*

The stuard hungeryd att þe last,

372 For he gaue hym nought.

The stuard satt ałł in a stody,

Hys lord hadde forgote curtesy :

375 Tho[1] seyd þe stuard, "geue me some." [¹ MS. *The*]

The lord seyd, " sorowe haue þe morsełł or sope

That schałł come in thy throte ! *and won't give*

378 Nott so much as o crome ! *him one crumb:*

Butt þou wylt helpe to dyght þis lyne, *let him work and*

Much hungyr yt schałł be thyne *earn some for*

  himself.

381 Though þou make much mone."

Vp he rose, and went therto, *The steward*

" Better ys me þus to doo *gives in,*

384 Whyle yt must nedys be do."

asks for work;
the wife throws
it him,

The stuard began fast to knocke,
The wyfe þrew hym a swyngelyng stocke,

387   Hys mete þerwyth to wyn);
Sche brought a swyngytt att þe last,
" Good syres," sche seyd, " swyngylle on fast :

390   For no þing that ye blynne."
Sche gaue hym⟩ a stocke to sytt vppon),
And seyd " syres, þis werke must nedys be done,

393   Att that that ys here yn)."

[leaf 183, back]

The stuard toke vp a stycke to saye,

and steward and
Lord are both
spinning away

" Sey, seye, swyngytt better yf ye may,

396   Hytt wytt be the better to spynne."
Were þe lord neuer so gret,

to earn their
dinner,

Yet was he fayne to werke for hys mete

399   Though he were neuer so sadde ;
Butt þe stuard þat was so stowde,
Was fayne to swyngelle þe scales owte,

402   Ther-of he was nott glad.

while the Lord's
people cannot
make out what has
become of him.

The lordys meyne þat were att home
Wyst nott where he was bycome,

405   They were futt sore adrad.

Then the Proctor
sees the wright

The proctoure of þe parysche chyrche rygtt
Came and lokyd on þe wryght,

408   He lokyd as he ware madde ;
Fast þe proctoure gan hym frayne,

and asks where
he got his gar-
land from.

" Where hadest þou þis garlond gayne ?

411   It ys euer lyke newe."
The wryght gan say " felowe,

" With my wife;

Wyth my wyfe, yf þou wylt knowe ;

414   That dare me nott rewe ;
For att the whyle my wyfe trew ys,

and while she is
true it will
never fade,

My garlond wolle hold hewe I-wys,

417   And neuer falle nor fade ;
And yf my wyfe take a paramoure,

but if she's false
it will."

Than wolle my garlond vade þe floure,

420   That dare I ley myne hede."

The proctoure þought, " in good faye

That schaⅡ I wete thys same daye

423   Whether yt may so be."

The proctor thinks he'll test this,

To the wryghtes hows he went,

He grete þe wyfe wyth feyre entente,

426   Sche seyd "syr, welcome be ye."

goes to the wright's wife

" A ! dame, my loue ys on you fast

Syth the tyme I sawe you last;

429   I pray you yt may so be

and declares his love for her;

That ye would graunt me of your grace

To play wyth you in some priuy place,

432   Or ellys to deth mutt me."

he must have her or die.

[leaf 184]

Fast þe proctoure gan to pray,

And euer to hym sche seyd "naye,

435   That wolle I nott doo.

She says nay,

Hadest þou done þat dede wyth me,

My spouse by hys garlond myght see,

438   That schuld torne me to woo."

as her husband will know of it by his garland.

The proctoure seyd, " by heuen kyng,

If he sey to the any þing

441   He schaⅡ haue sorowe vn-sowte;

The proctor

Twenty marke I wolle þe geue,

It wolle þe helpe welle to lyue,

444   The mony here haue I brought."

offers her 20 marks.

Nowe hath sche the tresure tane,

And vp þe steyre be they gane,

447   (What helpyth yt to lye?)

These she takes;

they go upstairs,

The wyfe went the steyre be-syde,

The proctoure went a lytyⅡ to wyde

450   He feⅡ downe by and by.

and the proctor tumbles into the cellar,

Whan he in to þe seller felle,

He wente to haue sonke in to helle,

453   He was in hart fuⅡ sory.

and thinks he is going to hell.

The stuard lokyd on the knyght,

And seyd "proctoure, for godes myght,

456   Come and sytt vs by."

The steward asks him to sit down;

The proctoure began to stare,

he doesn't know
where he is,

For he was he wyst neuer whare,

459   Butt wele he knewe þe knyght

And the stuard þat swyngelyd þe lyne.

but asks what
the Lord and
steward are
after there,

He seyd " syres, for godes pyne,

462   What do ye here thys nyght ? "

The stuard seyd, " god geue the care,

Thowe camyst to loke howe we fare,

465   Nowe helpe þis lyne were dyght."

He stode styll in a gret þought,

What to answer he wyst noght :

468   " By mary full of myght,"

working the
wife's flax;

The proctoure seyd, " what do ye in þis yne

For to bete thys wyfees lyne ?

[leaf 184, back] 471   For Ihesus loue, ffull of myght,"

The proctoure seyd ryght as he þought.

he, the proctor,
will never do
the like,

" For me yt schall be euyll wrought

it's not his trade.

474   And I may see aryght,

For I lernyd neuer in lond

For to haue a swyngell in hond

477   By day nor be nyght."

The steward says,
"We're as good
as you, and yet

The stuard seyd, " as good as þou

We hold vs that be here nowe,

480   And lett preue yt be syght ;

have to work for
our food."

Yet must vs worke for owre mete,

Or ellys schall we none gete,

483   Mete nor drynke to owre honde."

The Lord says,
" And you'll have
to work ere
you go."

The lord seyd, " why flyte ye two ?

I trowe ye wyll werke or ye goo,

486   Yf yt be as I vndyrstond."

Abowte he goys twyes or thryes ;

They eat and
drink, and give
the proctor
nothing,

They ete & drunke in such wyse

489   That þey geue hym ryght noght.

The proctoure seyd, " thynke ye no schame,

to his great
disgust,

Yheue me some mete, (ye be to blame,)

492   Of that the wyfe ye brought."

The stuard seyd " euyll spede the soppe

If eny morcell come in thy throte

495   Butt þou w*yth* vs hadest wrought."

The proctoure stode in a stody   *till at last*

Whether he mygħt worke hem by ;

498   And so to torne hys þougħt,

To the lord he drewe nere,

And to hym seyd w*yth* myld[*e*] chere,

501   " That mary mott the spede ! "

The proctoure began to knocke,   *he too knocks for*

The good wyfe rawte hym a rocke,   *work,*

504   For therto hadde sche nede ;

Sche seyd " whan I was mayde att home,

Other werke cowde I do none

507   My lyfe ther-wyth to lede."

Sche gaue hym in hande a rocke hynde,   *gets a distaff and*

And bade hem fast for to wynde   *some winding to do,*

510   Or ellys to lett be hys dede.   *[leaf 185]*

" Yes, dame," he seyd, " so haue I hele,

I schaħt yt worke both feyre & welle

513   As ye haue taute me."

He wauyd vp a strycke of lyne,

And he span wele and fyne   *and spins away well.*

516   By-fore the swyngeħt tre.

The lord seyd " þou spynnest to grete,

Therfor þou schalt haue no mete,

519   That þou schalt weħt see."

Thus þey satt and wrought fast   *Thus they all*

Tyħt þe wekedayes were past ;   *sit and work till the wright comes home.*

522   Then the wryght, home came he,

And as he cam by hys hows syde   *As he approaches*

He herd[1] noyse that was nott ryde   *he hears a noise,*

                                              [1 ? MS. hard]

525   Of p*er*sons two or thre ;

One of hem knockyd lyne,

A-nothyr swyngelyd good and fyne

528   By-fore the swyngyħt tre,

The thyrde did rele and spynne,

Mete and drynke ther-wyth to wynne,

531   Gret nede ther-of hadde he.

Thus þe wryght stode herkenyng ;

his wife comes to meet him,
Hys wyfe was ware of hys comyng,

534   And ageynst hym went sche.

" Dame," he seyd, " what ys þis dynne ?

and he asks what all that noise is about.
I here gret noyse here wythynne ;

537   Telł me, so god the spede."

" Why, three workmen have come to help us, dear.
" Syr," sche seyd, " workemen thre

Be come to helpe you and me,

540   Ther-of we haue gret nede ;

Who are they ?"
Fayne would I wete what they were."

The wright sees his Lord in the pit,
Butt when he sawe hys lord there,

543   Hys hert bygan to drede :

To see hys lord in þat place,

He þought yt was a strange cas,

and asks how
546   And seyd, " so god hym spede,

[leaf 185, back]
What do ye here, my lord and knygħt ?

Telł me nowe for godes mygħt

he came there.
549   Howe cam thys vn-to ?"

The knyght seyd " What ys best rede ?

The Lord asks mercy : he is very sorry.
Mercy I aske for my mysdede,

552   My hert ys wondyr wo."

" So am I," says the wright, " to see you among the flax and hemp,"
" So ys myne, veramen̄t,

To se you among thys flex and hempe,

555   Fulł sore yt ruytħ me ;

To se you in such hevynes,

Fulł sore myne hert yt doth oppresse,

558   By god in trinite."

and orders his wife to let the Lord out. " No, bother my snout if I do," says the wife, " before his lady sees what he wanted to do with me."
The wryght bade hys wyfe lett hym̄ owte,

" Nay, þen sorowe come on my snowte

561   If they passe hens to-daye

Tyłł that my lady come and see

Howe þey would haue done wyth me,

564   Butt nowe late me saye."

So she sends for the dame to fetch her lord home,
Añon sche sent after the lady bryght

For to fett home her lord and knyght,

567   Therto sche seyd nogħt ;

Sche told her what they hadde ment,

And of ther purpos & ther intente
570   That they would haue wrought.
Glad was þat lady of that tydyng ;
When sche wyst her lord was lyuyng,
573   Ther-of sche was fułł fayne : ·
Whan sche came vn-to þe steyre abouen),
Sche lokyd vn-to þe seller downe,
576   And seyd,—þis ys nott to leyne,—
" Good syres, what doo you here ? "
" Dame, we by owre mete fułł dere,
579   Wyth gret trauayle and peyne ;
I pray you helpe þat we were owte,
And I wyłł swere wyth-owtyn dowte
582   Neuer to come here agayne."
The lady spake the wyfe vn-tylle,
And seyd " dame, yf yt be youre wylle,
585   What doo thes meyny here ? "
The carpentarys wyfe her answerd sykerly,
" Ałł they would haue leyne me by ;
588   Euerych, in ther manere,
Gold and syluer they me brought,
And forsoke yt, and would yt noght,
591   The ryche gyftes so clere.
Wyllyng þey were to do me schame,
I toke ther gyftes wyth-owtyn blame,
594   *And* ther they be ałł thre."
The lady answerd her anon),
" I haue thynges to do att home
597   Mo than two or thre ;
I wyst my lord neuer do ryght noght
Of no þing þat schuld be wrought,
600   Such as fallyth to me."
The lady lawghed and made good game
Whan they came owte ałł in-same
603   From the swyngyłł tre.
The knyght seyd " felowys in fere,
I am glad þat we be here,

and tells her what he and his companions came there for.
The lady

looks down into the cellar, and says, " Good sirs, what are you doing ? "

" Earning our meat full dear :

help us out, and I'll never come here again."

The lady asks the wife why [leaf 186] the men are there.

The wife says they wanted to lie with her, and offered her gold and silver :

she took their gifts, and there they are.

The lady says she really wants her lord for herself,

and laughs heartily when the three culprits come out.

The Lord says,

606 By godes dere pyte ;

" Ah, you'd have
worked too if
you'd been
with us,

Dame, and ye hadde bene wyth vs,

Ye would haue wrought, by swete Ihesus,

609 As welle as dyd we."

And when they cam vp abouen)

They turnyd abowte and lokyd downe,

612 The lord seyd, " so god saue me,

I never had such
a turn in my life
before, I can tell
you."

Yet hadde I neuer such a fytte

As I haue hadde in þat lowe pytte ;

615 So mary so mutt me spede."

Then the Lord
and lady go
home,

The knyght and thys lady bryght,

Howe they would home that nyght,

618 For no thyng they would abyde ;

And so they went home ;

as ADAM of
COBSAM says.
[leaf 186, back]
On their
way home

Thys seyd Adam of Cobsam.[1]

621 By the weye as they rode

Throwe a wode in ther playeng,

For to here the fowlys syng

they halt,

624 They hovyd stylle and bode.

and the steward
and proctor
swear they'll
never go back for
five and forty
years.

The stuard sware by godes ore,

And so dyd the proctoure much more,

627 That neuer in ther lyfe

Would they no more come in þat wonne

Whan they were onys thens come,

630 Thys forty yere and fyve.

Of the tresure that they brought,

The lady gives
all their money to
the wright's wife.

The lady would geue hem ryght noght,

633 Butt gaue yt to the wryghtes wyfe.

The garland is
fresh as ever.

Thus the wryghtes garlond was feyre of hewe,

And hys wyfe bothe good and trewe :

636 There-of was he full blythe ;

I take wytnes att gret and small,

Thus true are all
good women
now alive !

Thus trewe bene good women all

639 That nowe bene on lyve,

So come thryste on ther hedys

[1] The letter between the *b* and *a* has had the lower part
marked over. But it must mean a long *ſ*.

Whan they mombyȜt on ther bedys
642   Ther pater noster ryue.

Here ys wretyn a geste of the wryght
That hadde a garlond weȜt I-dyght,
645   The coloure wyȜt neuer fade.

Here then is
written a tale
of the Wright and
his Garland.

Now god, þat ys heuyn kyng,
Graunt vs aȜt hys dere blessyng
648   Owre hertes for to glade ;

God grant us all
his blessing,

And aȜt tho that doo her husbondys ryȜt,
Pray we to Ihesu fuȜt of myght,
651   That feyre mott hem byfalle,

and may all true
faithful wives

And that they may come to heuen blys,
For thy dere moderys loue ther-of nott to mys,
654   Alle good wyues alle.

come to heaven's
bliss,

Now alle tho that thys tretys hath hard,
Ihesu graunt hem, for her reward,
657   As trew louers to be

and be such

As was the wryght vn-to hys wyfe
And sche to hym duryng her lyfe.
660   Amen, for charyte.

true lovers as the

[leaf 187]

wright and his
wife were.
Amen !

Here endyth the wryghtes processe trewe
Wyth hys garlond feyre of hewe
663   That neuer dyd fade the coloure.

Here ends our
tale of the
Garland

It was made, by the avyse
Of hys wywes moder wytty and wyse,
666   Of flourys most of honoure,

which was made
of White Roses,

Of roses whyte þat wyȜt nott fade,
Whych floure aȜt ynglond doth glade,
669   Wyth trewloues medelyd in syȜt ;

the flowers that
gladden all
England,

Vn-to the whych floure I-wys
The loue of god and of the comenys
672   Subdued¹ bene of ryȜt.

and receive the
love of God, and
of the Com-
mons too.

Explicit.

¹ May be *subdied ;* the word has been corrected.

NOTES.

The two first of the three operations of flax-dressing described in lines 526—529, p. 15,

> One of hem knockyd lyne,
> A-nothyr swyngelyd good and fyne
> By-fore the swyngyll-tre,
> The thyrde did rele and spynne,

must correspond to the preliminary breaking of the plant, and then the scutching or beating to separate the coarse tow or hards from the tare or fine hemp. Except so far as the *swingle* served as a heckle, the further *heckling* of the flax, to render the fibre finer and cleaner, was dispensed with, though heckles (iron combs) must have been in use when the poem was written—inasmuch as *hekele, hekelare, hekelyn,* and *hekelynge,* are in the Promptorium, ab. 1440 A.D. Under *Hatchell,* Randle Holme gives a drawing of a heckle.

The lines through the *h*'s in the MS. are not, I believe, marks of contraction. There are no insettings of the third lines, or spaces on changes of subject, in the MS.

For reference to two analogous stories to that of the Poem, I am indebted to Mr Thomas Wright. The first is that of *Constant Duhamel* in the third volume of Barbazan, and the second that of the Prioress and her three Suitors in the Minor Poems of Dan John Lydgate, published by the Percy Society, ed. Halliwell.

In the Barbazan tale "the wife is violently solicited by three suitors, the priest, the provost, and the forester, who on her refusal persecute her husband. To stop their attacks she gives them appointments at her house immediately after one another, so that when one is there and stripped for the bath, another comes, and, pretending it is her husband, she conceals them one after another in a large tub full of feathers, out of which they can see all that is going on in the room. She then sends successively for their three wives to come and bathe with her, the bath being still in the same room, and as each is stripped naked in the bath, she introduces her own husband, who dishonours them one after another, one *à l'enverse,* with rather aggravating circumstances, and all in view of their three husbands. Finally the latter are turned out of the house naked, or rather well feathered, then hunted by the whole town and their dogs, well bitten and beaten."

(If any one wants to see a justification of the former half of the proverb quoted by Roberd of Brunne,

> Frenche men synne yn lecherye
> And Englys men yn enuye,

let him read the astounding revelation made of the state of the early French mind by the tales in the 3rd and 4th vols. of Barbazan's Fabliaux, ed. 1808.)

The second story, told by Lydgate, is as follows :—A prioress is wooed by "a young knyght, a parson of a paryche, and a burges of a borrow." She promises herself to the first if he will lie for a night in a chapel sewn up in a sheet like a corpse; to the second, if he will perform the funeral service over the knight, and bury him ; to the third, if he will dress up like a devil, and frighten both parson and knight. This the burges Sir John does well, but is himself terrified at the corpse getting up: all three run away from one another : the knight falls on a stake, and into a snare set for bucks, and breaks his fore top in falling from the tree ; the merchant gets tossed by a bull ; the parson breaks his head and jumps into a bramble bush ; and the prioress gets rid of them all, but not before she has made the "burges" or "marchaunt" pay her twenty marks not to tell his wife and the country generally of his tricks.—*Minor Poems,* p. 107—117, ed. 1840.

GLOSSARY.

And, 89, 292, if.

Bayne, 348, ready.

Blynne, 4, cease, stop; AS. *blinnan.*

Blyue, 44, 110, 118, speedily.

Bonde, 226, a bund-le; Du. *bondt,* a bavin, a bush of thornes.

Brayne, 342, scull.

Broke 165, enjoy. AS. *brúcan,* Germ. *brauchen.* H. Coleridge.

Brydalle, 71, AS. *brýd-ál,* bride ale, marriage feast.

By, 197, buy.

Chaste, 176, chest, box, pit.

Dowte, 14, fear.

Dyght, 323, 379, prepare, dress.

Fare, 148, 324, going on, wish, project.

Fere, 604, company.

Flyte, 484, wrangle, quarrel; AS. *flít,* strife, wrangling.

Forthynketh, 51, repents, makes sorry; AS. *forþencan,* to despair.

Frayne, 409, ask; AS. *fregnan,* Goth. *fraihnan.*

Gan, 22, did.

Geue to God a gyfte, 351, I make a vow, I promise you, I'll take my oath.

Hele, 140, salvation.

Hovyd, 624, halted, stopt.

Hynde, 508? natty; *hende,* gentle.

I-doo, 335, done, finished.

I-dyght, 644, prepared.

In-same, 602, together.

Layne, 68, hide, conceal.

Lende, 107, stay; ?AS. *landian,* to land, or *lengian,* to prolong.

Leyne, 231, lay, beat.

Lyne, 214, AS. *lín,* flax; ?rope, 246.

Meyne, 403, household.

Myster, 12, trade; Fr. *mestier.*

O, 329, one.

Onredde, 308; AS. *unrét, unrót,* uncheerful, sorrowful, or *unréd,* imprudent.

Oþre, 205, second.

Putry, 61, adultery; O.Fr. *puterie,* whoring.

Rawte, 503, reached, gave.

Rewe, 186, have pity.

Rocke, 503, 508; Du. *een Rocke, Spinrock,* A Distaffe, or a Spinrock; *Rocken,* To Winde Flaxe or Wool upon a Rock (Hexham). Dan. *rok,* O.N. *rokkr,* G. *rocken:* "a distaff held in the hand from which the thread was spun by twirling a ball below. 'What, shall a woman with a *rokke* drive thee away?'" Digby Mysteries, p. 11 (Halliwell). "An Instrument us'd in some Parts for the spinning of Flax and Hemp." Phillips; for reeling and spinning (l. 529).

Rought, 198, AS. *róhte,* p. of *récan,* to reck, care for.

Ryde, 524, light, small, AS. *geryd,* levis, æquus. Lye.

Ry e, 642, Du. *rijf*, rife, or abundant.

Scales, 401 ; ? husks, bark, or rind, see *shoves**, in *Swyngylle*, below.

Schent, 258, destroyed ; AS. *scendan.*

Stounde, 4, short time,

Strycke, 514, " *Strike of Flax,* is as much as is heckled at one Handful." Phillips.

Swyngylle, 216, " Swingle-Staff, a Stick to beat Flax with," Phil. ; AS. *swingele,* a whip, lash. " To *swingle,* to beat; a Term among Flax-dressers." Phillips. Though Randle Holme, Bk. III., ch. viii. No. xxxiii., gives the *Swingle-Tree* of a Coach-Pole (these are made of wood, and are fastened by Iron hooks, stables (*sic*) chains and pinns to the Coach-pole, to the which Horses are fastened by their 'Harnish when there is more then two to draw the Coach), yet at Chap. vi., § iv., p. 285, col. 1, he says, " He beareth Sable, a *Swingle* Hand erected, Surmounting of a *Swingle* Foot, Or. This is a Wooden Instrument made like a Fauchion, with an hole cut in the top of it, to hold it by : It is used for the clearing of Hemp and Flax from the large broken Stalks or * Shoves, by the help of the said *Swingle* Foot, which it is hung upon, which said Stalks being first broken, bruised, and cut into shivers by a Brake. S. 3, such erected in Fesse O. born by *Flaxlowe*. S. 3, such in Pale A., born by *Swingler*."
(A drawing is given by Holme, No. 4, on the plate opposite p. 285.)
" *Swingowing* is the beating off the bruised inward stalk of the Hemp or Flax, from the outward pill, which as (*sic*) the Hemp or Flax, p. 106, col. 2.
Spinning is to twist the Flax hairs into Yarn or Thrid. *Reeling* is to wind the Yarn of the Wheel Spool on a Reel," p. 107, Col. 2.

Take, 161, deliver.

The, 187, thrive.

Tolle, 62, entice (H. H. Gibbs).

Tre, 105, wood, timber.

Trewloves, 669, either figures like true-lovers' knots, or the imitations of the herb or flower *Truelove*, which is given by Coles as *Herb Paris* (a quatrefoil whose leaves bear a sort of likeness to a true-lovers' knot), and in Halliwell as *one-berry :* but I cannot find that Edward IV. had any such plants on his arms or badge. Knots were often worn as badges, see Edmonston's Heraldry, Appendix, Knots. On the other hand, Willement (Regal Heraldry) notices that the angels attending Richard II. in the picture at Wilton, had collars worked with white roses and broom-buds ; and trueloves, if a plant be meant by it, may have been Edward's substitute for the broom (*planta genista*). The Trewloves bear, one, Ar. on a chev. sa., three cinquefoils, or ; the other, Ar. on a chev. sa., a quatrefoil of the field.

Vade,[1] 125, 419, fade ; Du. *vadden* (Hexham).

Wone, 275, store, quantity.

Wonne, 90, 628, dwelling.

Woode, 153, wild, mad.

Yheue, 491, give.

Yougeth, 20, youth, bachelor's freedom.

[1] The use of the flat *v*ade (l. 419, p. 12) within 2 lines of the sharp *f*ade (l. 417), corresponds with the flat 'stow*d*e,' l. 400, p. 12, riming with 'owte,' l. 401, ba*dd*e with ha*tt*e, l. 265-6. *C*ost, *b*rest, l. 142-3, are careless rimes too.

WOMEN.

[*Lambeth MS.* 306, *leaf* 135.]

Women, women, loue of women,
make bare purs with some men,
Some be nyse as a nonne hene,[1]
4   ʒit al thei be nat soo.
      some be lewde,
      some all be schrewde ;
    Go schrewes wher thei goo.

8 Sum̄ be nyse, and some be fonde,
    And some be tame, y vndirstonde,
    And some cane take brede of a manes hande,[2]
    Yit all thei be nat soo.
12   [Some be lewde, &c.]

Some cane part with-outen hire,   [leaf 135, back]
    And some make bate in eueri chire,
    And some cheke mate with oure Sire,
16   Yit all they be nat so.
      Some be lewde,
      and sume be schreuede,
    go wher they goo.

---

[1] The Rev. J. R. Lumby first told me of the proverb 'As white as a nun's hen,' the nuns being famous, no doubt, for delicate poultry. John Heywood has in his *Proverbes*, 1562 (first printed, 1546), p. 43 of the Spencer Society's reprint, 1867,

    She tooke thenterteinment of the yong men
    All in daliaunce, *as nice as a Nun's hen.*

The proverb is quoted by Wilson in his *Arte of Rhetorique,* 1553 (Hazlitt's *Proverbs*, p. 69).

[2] For *honde.*

20   Som be browne, and some be whit,
        And some be tender as a ttripe,
        And some of theym be chiry ripe,
          Yit all thei be not soo.
24   Sume be lewde,
          and some be schrewede,
       go wher they goo.

        Some of them be treue of love
28   Beneth þe gerdell, but nat above,
        And in a hode aboue cane chove,
          Yit all thei do nat soo.
          Some be lewde,
32   and some be schreude,
       go where they goo.

        Some cane whister, & some cane crie,
        Some cane flater, and some can lye,
36   And some cane sette þe moke awrie,
          Yit all thei do nat soo.
          Sume be lewde,
          and sume be schreuede,
40   go where thei goo.

        He that made this songe full good,
        Came of þe north and of þe sothern blode,
        And some-what kyne to Robyn Hode,
44   Yit all we be nat soo.
          Some be lewde,
          and some be schrewede,
       go where they goo.

48   Some be lewde, some be [s]chrwde,
        Go where they goo.

Explicit.

P.S.—This Poem was printed by Mr Halliwell in *Reliquiæ Antiquæ*, vol. i.,
p. 248, and reprinted by Mr Thomas Wright, at p. 103 of his edition of *Songs
and Carols* for the Percy Society, 1847. As, besides minor differences, the
reprint has *manne*, and the original *nanne*, for what I read as *nonne*, l. 3,
while both have *withowte* for *with oure*, l. 15, and *accripe* for *a ttripe*, l. 21
(see Halliwell's Dictionary, "*accripe*, a herb ?"), I have not cancelled this
impression. The other version of the song, from Mr Wright's MS. in his text,
pp. 89—91, differs a good deal from that given above.

Early English Text Society.

SUPPLEMENT

TO

The Wright's Chaste Wife.

ORIGINAL SERIES, No. 12; 1865.

ADDITIONAL ANALOGS

TO

The Wright's Chaste Wife

BY

W. A. CLOUSTON.

ADDITIONAL ANALOGUES

OF

"THE WRIGHT'S CHASTE WIFE."

By W. A. CLOUSTON.

THE numerous versions of this old and wide-spread story should be divided into two groups: I. Those in which there is a test of chastity, and the lovers are entrapped; II. Those in which there is no such test, but the suitors are (*a*) entrapped, or (*b*) engaged to perform unpleasant or dangerous tasks.

I. It is probable that some oral version of *The Wright's Chaste Wife* suggested to Massinger the plot of his comedy of *The Picture* (printed in 1630): Mathias, a Bohemian knight, about to go to the wars, expresses to his confidant Baptista, a great scholar, his fears lest his wife Sophia, on whom he doated fondly, should prove unfaithful during his absence. Baptista gives him a picture of his wife, saying:

> "Carry it still about you, and as oft
> As you desire to know how she's affected,
> With curious eyes peruse it. While it keeps
> The figure it has now entire and perfect
> She is not only innocent in fact
> But unattempted; but if once it vary
> From the true form, and what's now white and red
> Incline to yellow, rest most confident
> She's with all violence courted, but unconquered;
> But if it turn all black, 'tis an assurance
> The fort by composition or surprise
> Is forced, or with her free consent surrendered."

On the return of Mathias from the wars, he is loaded with rich gifts by Honoria, the wife of his master Ferdinand, king of Hungary; and when he expresses his desire to return to his fair and virtuous wife, Honoria asks him if his wife is as fair as she, upon which he shows her the picture. The queen resolves to win his love—merely to gratify her own vanity—and persuades him to remain a month at court. She then despatches two libertine courtiers to attempt the virtue of Mathias' wife. They tell her Mathias is given to the society of strumpets—moreover, not young, but old and ugly ones; so poor Sophia begins to waver.   Meanwhile the queen makes advances to Mathias, which at first he rejects; but afterwards, seeing a change in his wife's picture, he consents, when the queen says she will think over it and let him know her decision.   Sophia, at first disposed to entertain her suitors' proposals, on reflection determines to punish their wickedness; and, pretending to listen favourably to one of them, she causes him to be stripped to his shirt and locked in a room, where he is compelled to spin flax (like the suitors in our story), or go without food.   The other fares no better, and the play concludes with the exposure of the libertines to the king and queen, their attendants, and the lady's husband.

The 69th chapter of the continental *Gesta Romanorum* (translated by Swan) is to the following effect:[1]   A carpenter receives from his mother-in-law a shirt, having the wonderful quality of remaining unsoiled so long as he and his wife were faithful to each other.   The emperor, who had employed him in the erection of a palace, is astonished to observe his shirt always spotless, and asks him the cause of it; to which he replies, that it is a proof of his wife's unsullied virtue.   A soldier, having overheard this, sets off to attempt the wife's chastity, but she contrives to lock him in a room, where she keeps him on bread and water.   Two other soldiers successively visit her on the same errand, and share their comrade's fate.   When the carpenter has finished his job, he returns home and shows the unsullied shirt to his wife, who in her turn exhibits to him the three soldiers, whom he sets free on their promising to reform their ways.

The general resemblance of our story to this *Gesta* version does not, I think, render it therefore certain, or even probable, that the latter is the source whence it was derived; since a test similar to that of the Garland (for which a shirt is substituted in the *Gesta*) occurs both in the Indian original and in an intermediate Persian form, which is of Indian extraction.

In the celebrated Persian story-book, Nakhshabí's *Túti Náma* (Tales of a Parrot), written about A.D. 1306, the wife of a soldier, on his leaving home to enter the service of a nobleman, gives him a nosegay which, she tells him, would remain in full bloom while she was faithful to him.   After some time, the nobleman inquired of the soldier how he managed to procure a fresh nosegay every day in midwinter, and was informed that its perennial bloom betokened his

[1] Here given somewhat more fully than in the additional postscript to the Preface to the second edition of *The Wright's Chaste Wife*, 1869.

wife's chastity. The nobleman sends one of his cooks to try to form an intimacy with the soldier's wife, but she craftily entraps him. A second cook is despatched to learn the fate of the first, and meets with a similar reception. At last the nobleman himself sets off with his attendants—among whom was the soldier—to visit the chaste wife. He is received by her with great courtesy, and his two cooks, dressed as female slaves, are made by the wife to wait upon him at supper. The happy soldier then returns his wife the nosegay, fresh and blooming as ever.

The oldest form of the story yet known is found in the great Sanskrit collection entitled *Kathá Sarit Ságara*[1] (Book II., ch. 13): A merchant named Guhasena is compelled to leave his wife, Devasmitá, for a season, on important business matters. The separation is very painful to both, and the pain is aggravated by fears on the wife's part of her husband's inconstancy. To make assurance doubly sure, Siva was pleased to appear to them in a dream, and giving them two red lotuses, the god said to them: "Take each of you one of these lotuses in your hand; and if either of you shall be unfaithful during your separation, the lotus in the hand of the other shall fade, but not otherwise." The husband set out on his journey, and arriving in the country of Katáha he began to buy and sell jewels there. Four young merchants, learning the purport of his lotus and the virtue of his wife, set off to put it to the proof. On reaching the city where the chaste Devasmitá resided, they bribe a female ascetic to corrupt the lady, so she goes to her house, and adopting the device of the little she-dog—see ch. xxviii. of Swan's *Gesta Romanorum*,[2]— which she pretends is her own co-wife in a former birth, re-born in that degraded form, because she had been over-chaste, and warns Devasmitá that such should also be her fate if she did not "enjoy herself" during her husband's absence. The wise Devasmitá said to herself: "This is a novel conception of duty; no doubt this woman has laid a treacherous snare for me," and so she said to the ascetic: "Reverend lady, for this long time I have been ignorant of this duty, so procure me an interview with some agreeable man." Then the

---

[1] 'Ocean of the Streams of Story,' written in Sanskrit verse, by Somadeva, towards the end of the 11th century, after a similar work, the *Vrihat Ka'há*, 'Great Story,' by Gunadhya, 6th century, of which no copy has hitherto been discovered. A complete translation of Somadeva's work, by Professor C. H. Tawney, with useful notes of variants and derivatives of the tales, has lately been published, in two vols., large 8vo, at Calcutta.

[2] Taken into the *Gesta*, probably from the *Disciplina Clericalis* of P. Alfonsus. The incident is also the subject of a *fabliau*, and occurs in all the Eastern versions of the *Book of Sindibád*.

ascetic said : " There are residing here some young merchants, who have come from a distant country, so I will bring them to you." The crafty old hag returns home delighted with the success of her stratagem. In the meantime Devasmitá resolves to punish the four young merchants. So calling her maids, she instructs them to prepare some wine mixed with *datura* (a stupefying drug), and to have a dog's foot of iron made as soon as possible. Then she causes one of her maids to dress herself to resemble her mistress. The ascetic introduces one of the young libertines into the lady's house in the evening, and then returns home. The maid, disguised as her mistress, receives the young merchant with great courtesy, and, having persuaded him to drink freely of the drugged wine till he became senseless, the other women strip off his clothes, and, after branding him on the forehead with the dog's foot, during the night push him into a filthy ditch. On recovering consciousness he returns to his companions, and tells them, in order that they should share his fate, that he had been robbed on his way home. The three other merchants in turn visit the house of Devasmitá, and receive the same treatment. Soon afterwards the pretended devotee, ignorant of the result of her device, visits the lady, is drugged, her ears and nose are cut off, and she is flung into a foul pond. In the sequel, Devasmitá, disguised in man's apparel, proceeds to the country of the young libertines, where her husband had been residing for some time, and, going before the king, petitions him to assemble all his subjects, alleging that there are among the citizens four of her slaves who had run away. Then she seizes upon the four young merchants, and claims them as her slaves. The other merchants indignantly cried out that these were reputable men, and she answered that if their foreheads were examined they would be found marked with a dog's foot. On seeing the four young men thus branded, the king was astonished, and Devasmitá thereupon related the whole story, and all the people burst out laughing, and the king said to the lady : " They are your slaves by the best of titles." The other merchants paid a large sum of money to the chaste wife to redeem them from slavery, and a fine to the king's treasury. And Devasmitá received the money, and recovered her husband ; was honoured by all men, returned to her own city, and was never afterwards separated from her beloved.

Tests of chastity such as those in the above stories are very common in our old European romances. In *Amadis de Gaul* it is a garland ; in *Perce Forest* it is a rose, which, borne by a wife or a maiden of immaculate virtue, retains its bloom, but withers if the wearer is unchaste. In *Tristram, Perceval, La Morte d'Arthur,* and *Ariosto,* the test is a cup, the wine in which is spilled by the unfaithful lover or wife who attempts to drink from it. In one of the *fabliaux* of the northern minstrels of France the test is a mantle, 'Le Manteau mal taille': an English rendering of this, entitled 'The Boy and the Mantle,' is found in Percy's *Reliques.* And in Spenser we have the girdle of Florimel.

II. To the first subdivision (*a*) of the second group of variants, in which there is no test of chastity, but the suitors are entrapped, belongs the *fabliau* in Barbazan, tom. iii., of 'Constant du Hamel, ou la Dame qui atrappa un Prêtre, un Prévost, et un Forestier,' an abstract of which will be found in the original notes to our story; also the old ballad of *The Friar well-fitted,* of which some account is furnished by Dr Furnivall in an additional Postscript to his Preface (Second Edition, 1869).[1]

In an imperfect MS. text of the *Book of the Thousand and One Nights,* brought from Constantinople by Wortley Montagu, and now in the Bodleian Library, Oxford, there are two versions: Nights 726-728, 'The Lady of Cairo and her Three Gallants,' and Nights 738-743, 'The Virtuous Woman of Cairo and her Four Suitors.' Dr Jonathan Scott has given a translation of the second of these in the sixth volume of his edition of the *Arabian Nights:* The lady is solicited by the judge, the collector-general of port-duties, the chief of the butchers, and a rich merchant. She makes an assignation with each

---

[1] For members of the E. E. T. S. who possess only the 1865 edition, it may be as well to reproduce Dr Furnivall's note here :

"With *The Wright's Chaste Wife* may also be compared the ballad of ' *The Fryer well-fitted;* or

> A Pretty jest that once befel,
> How a maid put a Fryer to cool in the well,'

printed ' in the Bagford Collection ; in the Roxburghe (ii, 172) ; the Pepys (iii. 145) ; the Douce (p. 85) ; and in *Wit and Mirth, an Antidote to Melancholy,* 8vo, 1682, also, in an altered form, in *Pills to Purge Melancholy,* 1707, i. 340, or 1719, iii. 325 ' ; and the tune of which, with an abstract of the story, is given in Chappell's *Popular Music,* i. 273-5. The Friar makes love to the maid ; she refuses him for fear of hell-fire.

> Tush, quoth the Friar, thou needest not doubt ;
> If thou wert in Hell, I could sing thee out.

So she consents if he'll bring her an angel of money. He goes home to fetch it, and she covers the well with a cloth. When he comes back and has given her the money, she pretends that her father is coming, tells the Friar to run behind the cloth, and down he flops into the well. She won't help him at first, because if he could sing her out of hell, he could clearly sing himself out of the well : but at last she does help him out, keeps his money because he's dirtied the water, and sends him home dripping along the street like a new-washed sheep."

at her own house—of course at different hours—and acquaints her
husband of her plan to punish them, and at the same time reap some
profit. The judge comes first, and presents her with a rosary of
pearls. She makes him undress, and put on a robe of yellow muslin,
and a parti-coloured cap—her husband all the time looking at him
through an opening in the door of a closet. Presently a loud knock
is heard at the street-door, and on the pretence that it is her husband,
the judge is pushed into an adjoining room. The three other suitors,
as they successively arrive, bring each a valuable present, and are
treated in like manner. The husband now enters, and the lady tells
him—to the consternation, doubtless, of the imprisoned suitors—that
in returning from the bazaar she had met four antic fellows, whom
she had a great mind to bring home with her for his amusement.
He affects to be vexed that she had not done so, since he must go
from home to-morrow. The lady then says they are, after all, in the
next room, upon which the husband insists on their being brought
before him, one after another. So the judge is dragged forth in his
absurd attire, and compelled to caper like a buffoon, after which he
is made to tell a story, and is then dismissed. The others, having in
turn gone through a similar performance, are also sent packing.

There is another Arabian version in the famous romance of the
Seven Vazírs, which now forms part of the *Thousand and One Nights*.
The wife of a merchant, during one of his journeys of business, had
a young man as a substitute, who happened one day to be engaged
in a street brawl, and was apprehended by the police. She dressed
herself in her richest apparel, and repaired to the walí, or chief of
the police, and begged him to release her 'brother,' who was her
only protector, and against whom hired witnesses had sworn falsely.
The walí, seeing her great beauty, consents, on condition that she
should receive him at her house. She appoints a certain evening,
and the walí, enraptured, gives her twenty dínars (about ten pounds
of our money), saying, "Expend this at the bath;" and so she left
the walí with his heart busy thinking of all her charms. In like
manner—to be brief—the lady arranges with the kází, or judge, the
vazír, or minister of state, and the hájib, or city governor, that they
should come to her the same evening, appointing, of course, a differ-
ent hour for each. She then goes to a joiner, and desires him to
make her a large cabinet with four compartments. The poor crafts-
man, also smitten with her beauty, asks, as his only reward, that he
should be permitted to spend an evening with her. "In that case,"
says she, "you must make a fifth compartment," and appointed an

hour for him to visit her, the same evening she had fixed for the four city officials. When the walí arrived, she feasted him abundantly, then taking off his robes, dressed him in gay-coloured clothes, and plied him with wine till he was intoxicated ; and when he had written an order to the jailor to release the young man, lo! there was a loud knocking at the gate. "Who is coming?" asks the walí, in alarm. "It is my husband," replies the lady; "get into this cabinet, and I will return presently and let you out." Thus, as they came, the crafty lady entraps the four dignitaries and the poor joiner. Having sent a servant to the prison with the walí's order, her lover soon arrived, and they both set off for another city, with all the valuables they could carry. In the morning the landlord of the house, finding the gate open, entered, and hearing voices from the cabinet was alarmed, and summoned the neighbours. The cabinet was carried to the palace of the sultan, who sent for carpenters and smiths, and caused it to be broken open, when lo! he discovered the walí, the kází, the vazír, the hájib, and the poor joiner in their fantastic dresses. And the sultan laughed till he almost fainted, and commanded the story to be written from first to last. Search was made for the lady and her lover, but they were never discovered.[1]

In the Persian romance entitled *Bahár-i Dánish*, or 'Spring of Knowledge,' by Ináyatu-'llah of Delhi, a lady named Gohera, whose husband was in the hands of the police, makes assignations with the kôtwal (chief of police) and the kází, one of whom is entrapped in a great jar, the other in a chest; and next morning she causes porters to carry them before the sultan, who orders them to be punished, and her husband to be set at liberty. And in the Persian tales of the 'Thousand and One Days' (*Hazár-yek Rúz*), by Mukhlis, of Ispahán (Day 146 ff.), Arúya, the virtuous wife of a merchant, entraps, with her husband's sanction, a judge, a doctor, and the city governor.

The story is known, in various forms, throughout India, where, indeed, it had its origin. In the *Indian Antiquary*, 1873, there is a translation by G. H. Damant, of a folk-tale of Dinajpur, entitled 'The Touchstone,' in the concluding portion of which a young woman consents to receive at her house the kôtwal at the first watch of the night; the king's counsellor at the second watch; the king's minister at the third watch ; and the king himself at the fourth watch. She smears the kôtwal with molasses, pours water on him, covers his whole body with cotton wool, and then secures him near the window.

---

[1] In the Bodleian MS. of *The Nights* referred to above, this story is told separately from the *Seven Vazírs.—Nights*, 726—728.

The counsellor is hidden under a mat; the minister behind a bamboo-screen; and when the king comes, last of all, and sees the frightful figure of the kôtwal in the window, he asks what it is, and she replies that it is a rákshasa (a species of demon), upon which the king, minister, and counsellor flee from the. house in dread of the monster. The kôtwal is then released, and makes the best of his way home in his hideous condition.

In Miss Stokes' charming *Indian Fairy Tales* (No. 28), a merchant's clever wife, during his absence, takes four hanks of thread to the bazaar to sell, and is accosted in turn by the kôtwal, the vazír, the kází, and the king, to each of whom she grants an interview at her house, at different hours, and contrives to entrap them into chests. In the morning she hires four stout coolies, who take the chests on their backs, and proceeding to the houses of her suitors, disposes of them to their sons for various sums of money, telling each that the chest contained something he would value far beyond the sum she asked. A very similar Bengalí version, 'Adi's Wife,' is given by Damant in the *Indian Antiquary*," vol. ix. p. 2. And there is a curious variant in Narrain Sawmy's *Select Tamil Tales*, Madras, 1839, in which Ramakistnan (an Indian Scogin or Tyl Eulenspiegel) entraps the rája and his domestic chaplain, whom he induces to disguise themselves as women, on the pretext that he would introduce them to the beautiful wife of a man who had lately come to lodge at his house. The jester having locked them, one after the other, in the same room, when they recognize each other they are much ashamed, and softly request to be let out, but this Ramakistnan does only after they have solemnly promised to forgive him a hundred offences every day.

We now come to a second Sanskrit form of the story in the *Kathá Sarit Ságara* (Book I. ch. 4), from which the foregoing Indian, Persian, and Arabian versions have evidently been adapted or imitated. The storyteller, Vararuchi, relates that before proceeding to Himálaya to propitiate Siva with austerities, he deposited in the hand of the merchant Hiranyadatta all his wealth for the maintenance of his family during his absence, at the same time informing his wife Upakosá of it, and he thus proceeds:

" Upakosá, on her part anxious for my success, remained in her own house, bathing every day in the Ganges, strictly observing her vow. One day, when spring had come, she being still beautiful, though thin and slightly pale, and charming to the eyes of men, like the streak of the new moon, was seen by the king's domestic chaplain while going to bathe in the Ganges, and also by the head magistrate, and by the prince's minister; and immediately they all became a target for the arrows of love. It happened, too, somehow or other, that she took a long time bathing that day, and as she was returning in the evening, the prince's minister laid violent hands on her; but she with great presence of mind said to him: 'Dear sir, I desire this as much as you, but I am of respectable family, and my husband is away from home. How can I act thus? Some one might perhaps see us, and then misfortune would befall you as well as me. Therefore you must come without fail to my house in the first watch of the night of the spring-festival, when the citizens are all excited [and will not observe you].' When she had said this, and pledged herself, he let her go; but as chance would have it, she had not gone many steps further before she was stopped by the king's domestic chaplain. She made a similar assignation with him also, for the second watch of the same night; and so he too was, though with difficulty, induced to let her go. But after she had gone a little further, up comes a third person, the head magistrate, and detains the trembling lady. Then she made a similar assignation with him also, for the third watch of the same night; and having by great good fortune got him to release her, she went home all trembling. Of her own accord she told her handmaids the arrangements she had made, reflecting, 'Death is better for a woman of good family, when her husband is away, than to meet the eyes of people who lust after beauty.' Full of these thoughts and regretting me, the virtuous lady spent that night in fasting, lamenting her own beauty.

" Early the next morning she sent a maidservant to the merchant Hiranyadatta to ask for some money in order that she might honour the Bráhmans. Then that merchant also came, and said to her in private: ' Show me love, and then I will give you what your husband deposited.' When she heard that, she reflected that she had no witness to prove the deposit of her husband's wealth, and perceived that the merchant was a villain; and so, tortured with sorrow and grief, she made a fourth and last assignation with him for the last watch of the same night; and so he went away. In the meanwhile she had prepared by her handmaids, in a large vat, lamp-black mixed with oil and scented with musk and other perfumes, and she made ready four pieces of rag anointed with it, and she caused to be made a large trunk with a fastening outside.

" So on that day of the spring-festival the prince's minister came in the first watch of the night in gorgeous array. When he had entered without being observed, Upakosá said to him: 'I will not receive you until you have bathed; so go in and bathe.' The simpleton agreed to that, and was taken by the handmaids into a secret, dark inner apartment. There they took off his under-garments and his jewels, and gave him by way of an under-garment a single piece of rag, and they smeared the rascal from head to foot with a thick coating of that lamp-black and oil, pretending it was an unguent, without his detecting it. While they continued rubbing it into every limb, the second watch of the night came, and the chaplain arrived; the handmaids thereupon said to the minister: 'Here is the king's chaplain come, a great friend of Vararuchi's, so creep into this box;' and they bundled him into the trunk, just as he was, all naked, with the utmost precipitation; and then they fastened it outside with a bolt. The priest too was brought inside into the dark room on the pretence of a bath, and was in the same way stripped of his garments and ornaments, and made a fool of by the handmaids by being rubbed with lamp-black and oil, with nothing but the piece of rag on him, until in the third watch the chief magistrate arrived. The handmaids immediately terrified the priest with the news of his arrival, and pushed him into the trunk like his predecessor. After they had bolted him in, they brought in the magistrate on the pretext of giving him a bath, and so he, like his fellows, with the piece of rag for his only garment, was bamboozled by being continually anointed with lamp-black, until in the last watch of the night the merchant arrived. The handmaids made use of his arrival to alarm the magistrate, and bundled him also into the trunk, and fastened it on the outside.

"So those three being shut up inside the box, as if they were bent on accustoming themselves to live in the hell of blind darkness, did not dare to speak on account of fear, though they touched one another. Then Upakosá brought a lamp into the room, and making the merchant enter it, said to him: 'Give me that money which my husband deposited with you.' When he heard that, the rascal, observing that the room was empty, said: 'I told you that I would give you the money your husband deposited with me.' Upakosá, calling the attention of the people in the trunk, said: 'Hear, O ye gods, this speech of Hiranyadatta.' When she had said this, she blew out the light; and the merchant, like the others, on the pretext of a bath was anointed by the handmaids for a long time with lamp-black. Then they told him to go, for the darkness was over, and at the close of the night they took him by the neck and pushed him out of the door sorely against his will. Then he made the best of his way home, with only the piece of rag to cover his nakedness, and smeared with the black dye, with the dogs biting him at every step, thoroughly ashamed of himself, and at last reached his own house; and when he got there, he did not dare to look his slaves in the face while they were washing off that black dye. The path of vice is indeed a painful one.

"In the early morning, Upakosá, accompanied by her handmaids, went, without informing her parents, to the palace of King Nanda, and there herself stated to the king that the merchant Hiranyadatta was endeavouring to deprive her of money deposited with him by her husband. The king, in order to inquire into the matter, immediately had the merchant summoned, who said: 'I have nothing in my keeping belonging to this lady.' Upakosá then said: 'I have witnesses, my lord. Before he went, my husband put the household gods into a box, and this merchant with his own lips admitted the deposit in their presence. Let the box be brought here, and ask the gods yourself.' Having heard this, the king in astonishment ordered the box to be brought. Thereupon in a moment that trunk was carried in by many men. Then Upakosá said: 'Relate truly, O gods, what that merchant said, and then go to your houses: if you do not, I will burn you, or open the box in court.' Hearing that, the men in the box, beside themselves with fear, said: 'It is true, the merchant admitted the deposit in our presence.' Then the merchant, being utterly confounded, confessed all his guilt. But the king, being unable to restrain his curiosity, after asking permission of Upakosá, opened the chest there in court by breaking the fastening, and those three men were dragged out, looking like three lumps of solid darkness, and were with difficulty recognised by the king and his ministers. The whole assembly then burst out laughing, and the king in his curiosity asked Upakosá what was the meaning of this; so the virtuous lady told the whole story. All present in court expressed their approbation of Upakosá's conduct, observing: 'The virtuous behaviour of women of good family, who are protected by their own excellent disposition only,[1] is incredible.' Then all those coveters of their neighbour's wife were deprived of all their living and banished from the country. Who prospers by immorality? Upakosá was then dismissed by the king, who showed his great regard for her by a present of much wealth, and said to her: 'Henceforth thou art my sister;' and so she returned home."

[1] Instead of being confined in the zenana, or harem. Somadeva wrote before the Muhammadan conquest of India.

Such is the fine story of the virtuous Upakosá, according to Professor Tawney's translation, of which the Arabian version in the *Seven Vazírs* is a rather clumsy imitation. But before attempting a comparison of the several versions, there remain to be adduced those of the second subdivision (*b*) of the group in which there is no magical test of chastity, and to which belongs Lydgate's metrical tale of *The Lady Prioress and her Three Wooers*, an abstract of which is cited by Dr Furnivall in the original notes to our story.

If Lydgate did not adapt his tale from Boccaccio (*Decameron*, Day IX., Nov. 1), both versions must have been derived from a common source. Boccaccio's story is to this effect : A widow lady in Pistoia had two lovers, one called Rinuccio, the other Alexander, of whom neither was acceptable to her. At a time when she was harassed by their importunities, a person named Scannadio, of reprobate life and hideous aspect, died and was buried. His death suggested to the lady a mode of getting rid of her lovers, by asking them to perform a service which she thought herself certain they would not undertake. She acquainted Alexander that the body of Scannadio, for a purpose she would afterwards explain, was to be brought to her dwelling, and that, as she felt a horror at receiving such an inmate, she offered him her love if he would attire himself in the dead garments of Scannadio, occupy his place in the coffin, and allow himself to be conveyed to her house in his stead. To Rinuccio she sent to request that he would bring the corpse of Scannadio at midnight to her habitation. Both lovers, contrary to her expectation, agree to fulfil her desires. During the night she watches the event, and soon perceives Rinuccio coming along, bearing Alexander, who was equipped in the shroud of Scannadio. On the approach of some watchmen with a light, Rinuccio throws down his burden and runs off, while Alexander returns home in the dead man's clothes. Next day each demands the love of his mistress, which she refuses, pretending to believe that no attempt had been made to fulfil her commands (*Dunlop*). Lydgate's story is a very great improvement on this of the illustrious Florentine : the Lady Prioress pretends the "corpse" had been arrested for debt; and the adventures of her three suitors are ingeniously conceived, and told with much humour.

Under the title of 'The Wicked Lady of Antwerp and her Lovers,' Thorpe, in his *Northern Mythology*, gives a story which is cousin-german to those of Boccaccio and Lydgate : A rich woman in Antwerp led a very licentious life, and had four lovers, all of whom visited her in the evenings, but at different hours, so that no one

knew anything of the others. The Long Wapper[1] one night assumed
the form of this lady. At ten o'clock came the first lover, and Long
Wapper said to him : " What dost thou desire ? "—" I desire you for
a wife," said the spark.—" Thou shalt have me," replied the Wapper,
" if thou wilt go instantly to the churchyard of our Lady, and there
sit for two hours on the transverse of the great cross."—" Good," said
he, " that shall be done," and he went and did accordingly. At half-
past ten came the second. " What dost thou want ? " asked the
Long Wapper.—" I wish to marry you," answered the suitor.—"Thou
shalt have me," replied the Wapper, " if thou wilt go previously to
the churchyard of our Lady, there take a coffin, drag it to the foot of
the great cross, and lay thyself in it till midnight."—" Good," said
the lover, " that shall be done at once," and he went and did so.
About eleven o'clock came the third. Him the Long Wapper com-
missioned to go to the coffin at the foot of the cross in our Lady's
churchyard, to knock thrice on the lid, and to wait there till midnight.
At half-past eleven came the fourth, and Wapper asked him what his
wishes were. " To wed you," answered he.—" Thou shalt do so,"
replied Wapper, " if thou wilt take the iron chain in the kitchen,
and dragging it after thee, run three times round the cross in the
churchyard of our Lady."—" Good," said the spark, " that I will do."
The first had set himself on the cross, but had fallen dead with
fright to the earth on seeing the second place the coffin at his feet.
The second died with fright when the third struck thrice on the
coffin. The third fell down dead when the fourth came rattling his
chain, and the fourth knew not what to think when he found his
three rivals lying stiff and cold around the cross. With all speed he
ran from the churchyard to the lady to tell her what had happened.
But she, of course, knew nothing of the matter ; when, however, on
the following day, she was informed of the miserable death of her
lovers, she put an end to her own life.

We have here a very curious and tragical version of the self-same
story which the Monk of Bury—or whosoever was the author—has
told so amusingly of the Lady Prioress and her Three Wooers. In
the Far North, where our story is also current, magical arts are
employed in punishment of importunate and objectionable suitors :
In the latter part of the tale of ' The Mastermaid ' (Dasent's
Popular Tales from the Norse), the heroine takes shelter in the hut
of a crabbed old crone, who is killed by an accident, and the maid

---

[1] A Flemish sprite, whose knavish exploits resemble those of our English
Robin Goodfellow.—*Thorpe.*

is thus left alone. A constable, passing by, and seeing a beautiful girl at the window, falls in love with her, and having brought a bushel of money, she consents to marry him; but at night, just when they have got into bed, she says that she has forgot to make up the fire; this the doting bridegroom undertakes to do himself, but no sooner has he laid hold of the shovel, than she cries out: "May you hold the shovel, and the shovel hold you, and may you heap burning coals over yourself till morning breaks!" So there stood the constable all night, heaping coals of fire on his own head till daybreak, when he was released from the spell, and ran home. In like manner, on the second night the damsel casts her spells over an attorney, who is made to hold the handle of the porch-door till morning; and on the third night the sheriff is compelled to hold the calf's-tail, and the calf's-tail to hold him, till morning breaks, when he goes home in sorry plight.—In an Icelandic version, the calf's-tail is the only device adopted by the young witch, but it proves equally efficacious for her purposes.

These are all the versions of this world-wide story with which I am at present acquainted: some of them are taken from the appendix to my privately-printed *Book of Sindibád*. Regarding the immediate source of Adam of Cobsam's diverting tale, I do not think that was the *Gesta* version, with which it corresponds only in outline; both were doubtless adapted independently from some orally-current form of the story. If we assume that the *Kathá Sarit Ságara* faithfully represents its prototype of the 6th century—the *Vrihat Kathá*—then for the elements of *The Wright's Chaste Wife* we must go to two different but cognate tales in that collection: for the garland as the test of chastity we have the lotus-flower in the story of Guhasena; and the entrapping of the suitors we find in the story of Upakosá. Of the Eastern versions cited, the prototype of *The Wright's Chaste Wife* is the story of the soldier's wife in the *Túti Náma*—a work, it is true, which does not date earlier than A.D. 1306, but it was derived from a much older Persian work of the same description, which again was based upon a Sanskrit story-book, of which the *Suka Saptati* (Seventy Tales of a Parrot) is the modern representative. The two stories in the *Vrihat Kathá*—or rather, portions of them—seem thus to have been fused into one at an early date, and reached Europe in a form similar to the *Gesta* and Adam of Cobsam's versions. But the story of Upakosá also found its way to Europe separately, and not through the Arabian versions assuredly, since these are much later than the times of the Trouvères. Moreover, the *fabliau* has preserved incidents of the Indian story, which are omitted in the Arabian versions, with comparatively little modification, namely : that of the bath—a common preliminary to farther intimacy in tales of gallantry; the smearing of the naked suitors with lamp-black and oil—they are 'feathered' in the *fabliau;* and the dogs snapping the heels of the roguish merchant.—That Boccaccio was not the inventor of his version seems evident, from the existence of analogous popular tales in Northern Europe.   Be this as it may, Adam of Cobsam's story has furnished us with a curious illustration of Baring-Gould's remark: "How many brothers, sisters, uncles, aunts, and cousins of all degrees a little story has! and how few of the tales we listen to can lay any claim to originality!"

GLASGOW, *April 1886.*

D7